INCREDIBLE
EARTH

Authors: Anita Ganeri, John Malam, Clare Oliver, Adam Hibbert and Denny Robson

Illustrators: John Butler, Jim Eldridge, James Field, Andrew & Angela Harland, Colin Howard, Rob Jakeway, Mike Lacey, Sarah Lees, Gilly Marklew, Dud Moseley, Terry Riley, Sarah Smith, Stephen Sweet, Mike Taylor, Ross Watton (SGA), Ian Thompson and Rob Shone

Cartoonist: Peter Wilks (SGA)

Consultant: Steve Parker

This edition designed by Design Principals and Starry Dog Books.

This edition published by Parragon in 2009

Parragon
Queen Street House
4 Queen Street
Bath BA1 1HE, UK

Copyright © Parragon Books Ltd 2001

Printed in Indonesia

British Library Cataloguing-in-Publication Data

A catalogue record for this book is available from the British Library.

ISBN 978-1-4075-7998-6

INCREDIBLE
EARTH

PaRragon

Bath · New York · Singapore · Hong Kong · Cologne · Delhi · Melbourne

Contents

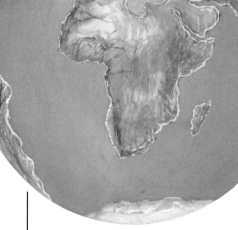

CHAPTER ONE

PREHISTORIC LIFE ON EARTH

How old is the Earth?

Earth is millions and millions of years old. In fact, our planet is four thousand six-hundred million years old. When the Earth's age (4.6 billion years) is written as a number, it looks like this: 4,600,000,000. It's hard for us to imagine anything so old.

Earth today

 Amazing! Some of Earth's oldest known rocks are found in Scotland. They are about 3.5 billion years old.

Fiery conditions on Earth before life began

Has there always been life on the Earth?

Nothing at all lived on the Earth for the first billion (1,000 million) years of the planet's existence. The conditions were not right for life. There were no plants or animals of any kind. Earth was a dangerous place where life could not survive.

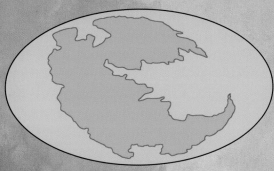
200 million years ago

150 million years ago

80 million years ago

 ## Has the Earth always looked the same?

These maps show how Earth's land and sea looked in the past. To fit everything on them, Earth has been drawn as an oval. For a long time, all land was joined together in one giant mass. Over millions of years it broke up into smaller pieces. They turned into today's continents.

 ## Is it true?
The continents are still moving.

YES. The continents move about 4 centimetres each year – the length of your little finger. Millions of years in the future, Earth will look very different from today.

11

? When and where did life on Earth begin?

Life on Earth began about 3.5 billion years ago. The first life appeared in the sea. It was born into a world that looked very different from today. The atmosphere was filled with poisonous gases. The sky was pink, and the sea was rusty-red.

Conditions on Earth were hostile when life first began

Is it true?
Earth is the only planet with life on it.

MAYBE. This is one of the greatest unsolved mysteries. Life probably does exist on other planets besides Earth, but nothing has been found so far. The search continues.

? How did life begin?

It is thought that life began when lightning hit the sea. Lightning sent energy into the water. Chemicals in the sea were mixed together by energy. New substances, called amino acids, were made, from which life was able to grow.

 Amazing! The first living things on Earth were so small you could fit thousands of them on the head of a pin.

Close-up of bacteria

? What were the first living things?

The first living things were bacteria. They lived in the sea. Some bacteria changed into algae, which were simple plants. Algae lived in the sea in masses, like huge blankets. They made oxygen, which helped to turn the sky and sea blue.

13

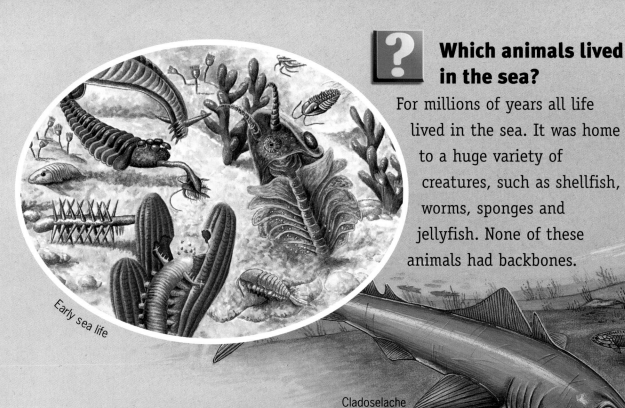

? Which animals lived in the sea?

For millions of years all life lived in the sea. It was home to a huge variety of creatures, such as shellfish, worms, sponges and jellyfish. None of these animals had backbones.

Early sea life

Cladoselache
(an early shark)

Is it true?
The very first fish didn't have jaws.

YES. Instead of jaws to open and close their mouths the very first fish sucked food into their mouths. They are called jawless fish.

Acanthodians

Heliobatis fossil

? Which animals first had backbones?

About 510 million years ago, new kinds of animals appeared in the sea. They were the first fish, and they were the first animals with backbones. Because they had backbones to support their bodies they could become much larger.

Amazing! In the Indian Ocean is a fish called a coelacanth. It has hardly changed for 350 million years. It is a living fossil.

Dunkleosteus

Cheirolepis

Placoderms

? What were early fish like?

Giant sharks, much larger than any alive today, swam through the oceans. They hunted smaller fish. Armoured fish grew bony plates to protect their soft bodies. Other fish had bodies covered in sharp spines.

Sacabambaspis

15

When did life first appear on land?

About 440 million years ago, the first life appeared on land. It was simple plant life, similar to today's mosses. Then, about 400 million years ago, the first land animals – worms, spiders, scorpions and insects – evolved as they moved on to the land.

Is it true?
There are no amphibians alive today.

NO. There are many different amphibians in the world today. Frogs, toads and salamanders are all amphibians.

Scorpion

Centipede

Cockroach

Why did some fish grow legs?

Some fish began to live in shallow water. It was difficult to swim in the shallows. To help these fish move around they grew short legs. Some of them also grew lungs, which meant they could breathe air. These animals could live in water and on land.

Acanthostega (an early amphibian)

Amazing! The lungfish is one of today's fish that can live out of water. It can breathe air.

Which animal lives in water and on land?

An animal that can live in water and on land is called an amphibian. It means 'double life'. The first amphibians appeared by 350 million years ago. Gradually, they spent more and more time on land.

Ichthyostega
(an early amphibian)

17

What are reptiles?

About 300 million years ago, some amphibians changed into reptiles. They could live on land all the time. Reptiles have backbones and scaly skin, and most lay eggs. Many reptiles, such as crocodiles, spend lots of time in the water, but they can't breathe underwater. They use the Sun to keep their bodies warm.

Is it true?
Some early reptiles had sails on their backs.

YES. Dimetrodon had a skin 'sail' on its back. It soaked up the Sun's heat, and controlled the animal's body temperature.

Hylonomus

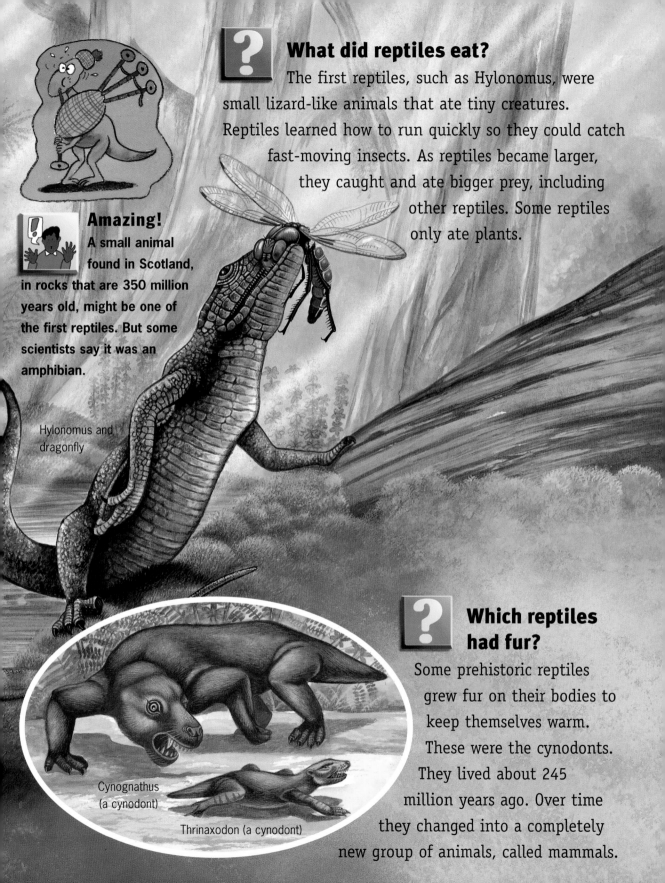

What did reptiles eat?

The first reptiles, such as Hylonomus, were small lizard-like animals that ate tiny creatures. Reptiles learned how to run quickly so they could catch fast-moving insects. As reptiles became larger, they caught and ate bigger prey, including other reptiles. Some reptiles only ate plants.

Amazing!
A small animal found in Scotland, in rocks that are 350 million years old, might be one of the first reptiles. But some scientists say it was an amphibian.

Hylonomus and dragonfly

Which reptiles had fur?

Some prehistoric reptiles grew fur on their bodies to keep themselves warm. These were the cynodonts. They lived about 245 million years ago. Over time they changed into a completely new group of animals, called mammals.

Cynognathus (a cynodont)

Thrinaxodon (a cynodont)

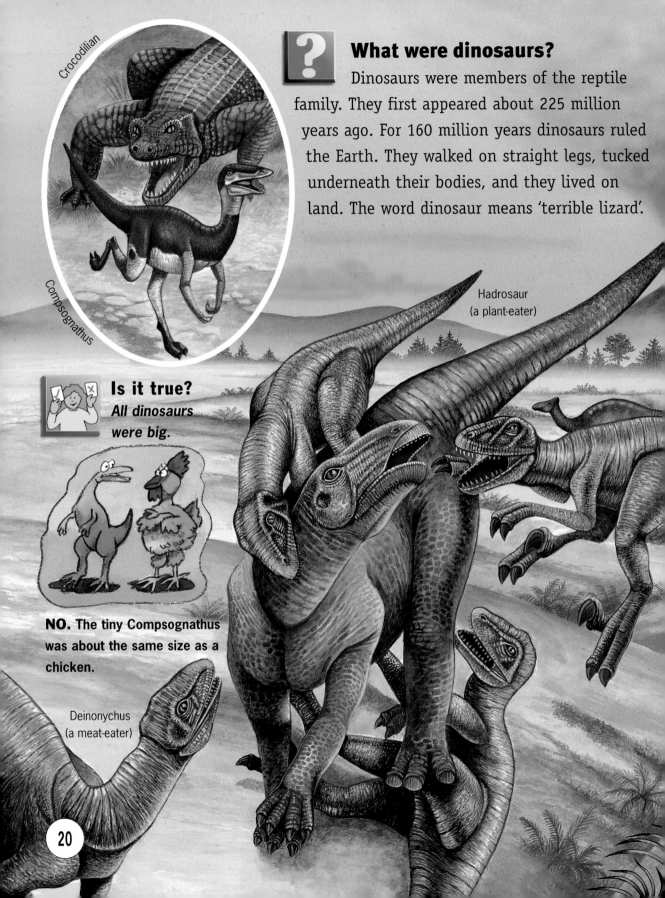

Crocodilian

Compsognathus

? What were dinosaurs?

Dinosaurs were members of the reptile family. They first appeared about 225 million years ago. For 160 million years dinosaurs ruled the Earth. They walked on straight legs, tucked underneath their bodies, and they lived on land. The word dinosaur means 'terrible lizard'.

Hadrosaur
(a plant-eater)

Is it true?
All dinosaurs were big.

NO. The tiny Compsognathus was about the same size as a chicken.

Deinonychus
(a meat-eater)

What did dinosaurs eat?

Some dinosaurs were carnivores. This means they ate meat and fish. Some were herbivores. These dinosaurs ate plants. A third group were omnivores. They had a mixed diet and ate both meat and plants. Some dinosaurs swallowed stones, which crushed food inside their stomachs so it was easier to digest.

Seismosaurus (a plant-eater)

Amazing! When Ankylosaurus filled its bony plates with blood it could have blushed pink!

What colour were dinosaurs?

No one knows what colour dinosaurs were. Perhaps some had skins that matched their surroundings, making them hard to see. Some might have had bright markings to attract mates, or scare others away.

Tyrannosaurus rex and Hysilophodons

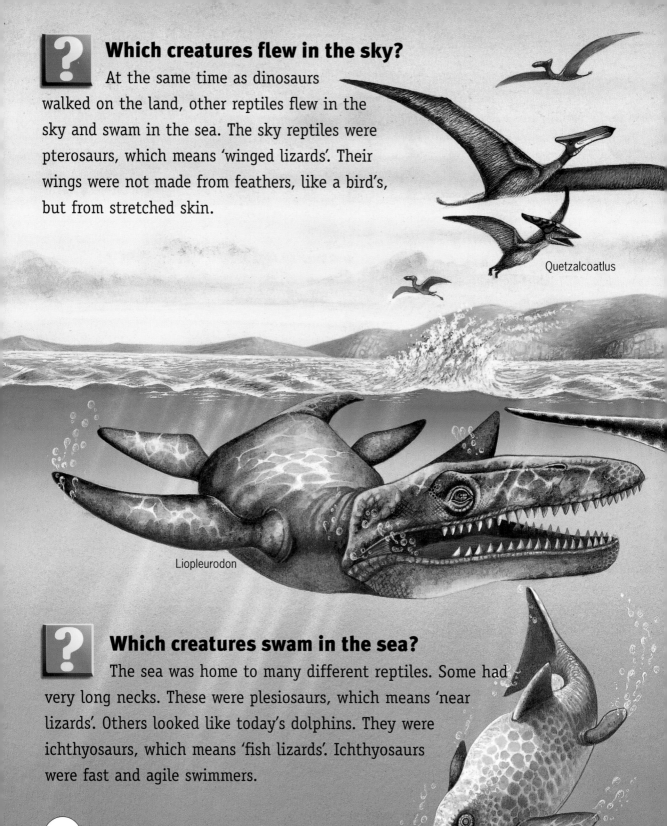

? Which creatures flew in the sky?

At the same time as dinosaurs walked on the land, other reptiles flew in the sky and swam in the sea. The sky reptiles were pterosaurs, which means 'winged lizards'. Their wings were not made from feathers, like a bird's, but from stretched skin.

Quetzalcoatlus

Liopleurodon

? Which creatures swam in the sea?

The sea was home to many different reptiles. Some had very long necks. These were plesiosaurs, which means 'near lizards'. Others looked like today's dolphins. They were ichthyosaurs, which means 'fish lizards'. Ichthyosaurs were fast and agile swimmers.

Ichthyosaur

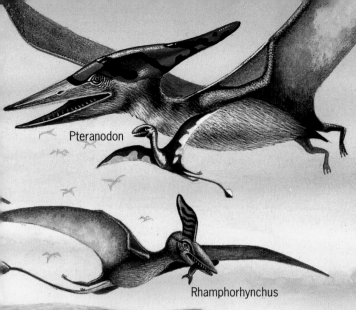

Pteranodon

Rhamphorhynchus

Is it true?

One pterosaur was as big as a small plane.

YES. Quetzalcoatlus was an enormous pterosaur. It had wings 12 metres across. It is the biggest flying creature ever.

Plesiosaur

? What did pterosaurs eat?

Some pterosaurs ate fish, which they scooped from the sea with their long beaks. Some pterosaurs may have held lots of fish inside their cheek pouches, as pelicans do today.

Amazing! The short-necked plesiosaur Liopleurodon grew to 23 metres and weighed 50 tonnes. It was a giant sea monster!

Feeding pterosaur

What are birds?

Birds are animals with backbones, they lay eggs, can make their own body heat, and have wings. They are also the only animals with feathers. Not all birds can fly. The first birds lived at the same time as the dinosaurs.

Prophaeton

Phororhacos

Is it true?

Ostrich eggs are the biggest eggs ever laid by a bird.

Hyracotherium (a very small, early kind of horse)

NO. The extinct bird Aepyornis laid the biggest eggs of all time. Each one was about the size of 150 hen's eggs.

Where do birds come from?

Birds evolved from small, meat-eating dinosaurs. Fossils show that some of these dinosaurs had feathers. They are called 'dinobirds'. The first 'dinobirds' probably could not fly.

Caudipteryx

Amazing!

Today's hoatzin bird, which lives in South America, has claws on its wings when young – just like Archaeopteryx, its prehistoric ancestor, did.

Archaeopteryx   Fossilised Archaeopteryx

Which was the first true bird?

The first true bird – a bird that could fly – appeared about 150 million years ago. It is known as Archaeopteryx, which means 'ancient wing'. It had claws on its wings.

25

? What are mammals?

Mammals have backbones, their bodies are covered in hair or bristles, they make their own body heat, and they feed their young on milk. They have larger brains than most other animals.

Early mammals

Megazostrodon

Ginkgo tree

? When did the first mammals appear?

The first mammals appeared on Earth about 220 million years ago. They lived at the same time as the dinosaurs. Mammals survived after the dinosaurs died out, and then they became the ruling animals on Earth. There are about 4,200 different kinds of mammals alive today.

❓ Did mammals only live on land?

Mammals came to live in all of Earth's habitats. Many lived on land, but some, such as bats, were able to glide through the air on wings of skin. Other mammals swam in the sea, such as whales, dolphins and seals.

Basilosaurus

! Amazing!
Woolly mammoths were big elephants with extra-long tusks up to 3 metres long. Their bodies were covered in fur.

Tyrannosaurus rex

Is it true?
The elephant is the largest land mammal ever to have lived.

NO. Indricotherium was the largest land mammal. It was almost 8 metres tall and as heavy as four elephants.

A group of human ancestors collecting fruit

Australopithecus skull

Who were our ancestors?

Our earliest ancestors were apes that walked upright on two legs. Australopithecus, meaning 'southern ape', was one of the first apes to walk upright. It lived at least three million years ago, and was short and hairy.

Is it true?
Lucy was very short.

YES. Compared with a modern human, an adult Australopithecus like Lucy was very short – about 1.2 metres tall.

How did they live?

Australopithecus probably lived in small family groups. These bands of human ancestors wandered across the grassy plains of their homeland. They ate fruit, leaves, seeds and roots. They may have used sticks to help dig for food, and may have eaten meat, too.

AFRICA

Australopithecus finds

Where did they live?

Australopithecus lived in Africa. Bones of this upright ape have been found in several countries, including Tanzania, Ethiopia and South Africa. Africa is where human species probably began, a few million years ago.

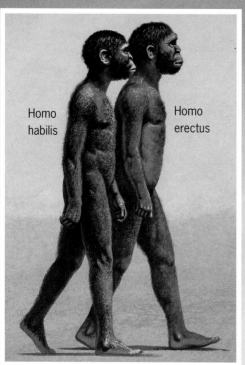

Homo habilis

Homo erectus

Who were the very first humans?

The first people we think of as humans appeared in Africa. About two million years ago, Homo habilis (handy man) appeared. Then, more than one million years ago, Homo erectus (upright man) appeared, but they weren't modern humans.

Amazing!

Homo erectus had fire. Fire provided warmth, gave heat for cooking, and offered protection from predators.

Hand axe

Fire-making tool

Flint knife

Did they have any tools?

Homo habilis was the first tool-user. This is why he is called 'handy man'. He made simple tools, such as choppers, from pebbles. The tools made by Homo erectus were better. He shaped stones into hand axes, and he was the first to use fire.

❓ What did they eat?

Homo habilis and Homo erectus ate meat and plants. Meat probably came from dead animals which they found. They may have hunted for some small animals. Plants gave them berries and leaves. They used stone tools to cut and scrape their food.

Homo erectus people hunted and gathered their food

Is it true?
Homo erectus was a wanderer.

YES. More than one million years ago, Homo erectus began to move out of Africa, travelling to Europe and Asia.

When did modern humans appear?

Just over 100,000 years ago Homo sapiens appeared. The name means 'wise man'. They were modern humans. In Europe they lived during the freezing Ice Age, a time when glaciers covered the land. The Ice Age ended 12,000 years ago.

Mammoth hunt

Is it true?
Homo sapiens have all died out.

NO. All people on Earth today are members of Homo sapiens. If they had died out, like other kinds of early human, none of us would be here today!

? Where did they live?

Homo sapiens first appeared in Africa, and from there, they spread out across the world. They lived in cave entrances, and in places sheltered by overhanging rocks. In the open they made huts from branches, covered with skins.

As the climate grew warmer, Homo sapiens people migrated across the world

Amazing! People who lived during the Ice Age played musical instruments. They made whistles from bones, and drums from shoulder-blades.

Animal carving

? Were they artists?

The humans who lived in Europe during the Ice Age were among the first artists. They painted pictures of horses, bison and deer on the walls of their caves. Bone and ivory were carved into figures of animals and people.

Cave painting

33

We find out about life in the past by looking for evidence. Fossils are one kind of evidence. They are the remains of living things that have been preserved. Objects made by humans, such as stone tools, are another kind of evidence.

A collection of fossils

Is it true?
Plants can't be fossilised.

NO. Plants can become fossils, in the same way that animals can. By studying them we learn about the plants that once grew on Earth.

1

2

3

4

How is a fossil made?
It takes millions of years to make a fossil. The pictures on the left show how it happens. (1) An animal dies. Its body sinks to the bottom of a lake. (2) Sand and silt cover its body. (3) The flesh rots away. Minerals seep into the bones and turn them to stone. The animal is now a fossil. (4) The fossil is found.

? Who looks for prehistoric life?

People who look for remains of prehistoric animals, such as dinosaurs, are called palaeontologists. People who look for ancient humans are archaeologists. They find great things, such as bones, tools, buildings, jewellery and weapons.

Palaeontologists excavating fossilised dinosaur bones

Amazing! A sticky resin that oozed from pine trees trapped insects that landed on it. It hardened into a substance called amber. Prehistoric insects are perfectly preserved inside it.

CHAPTER TWO

DINOSAURS

AND OTHER PREHISTORIC REPTILES

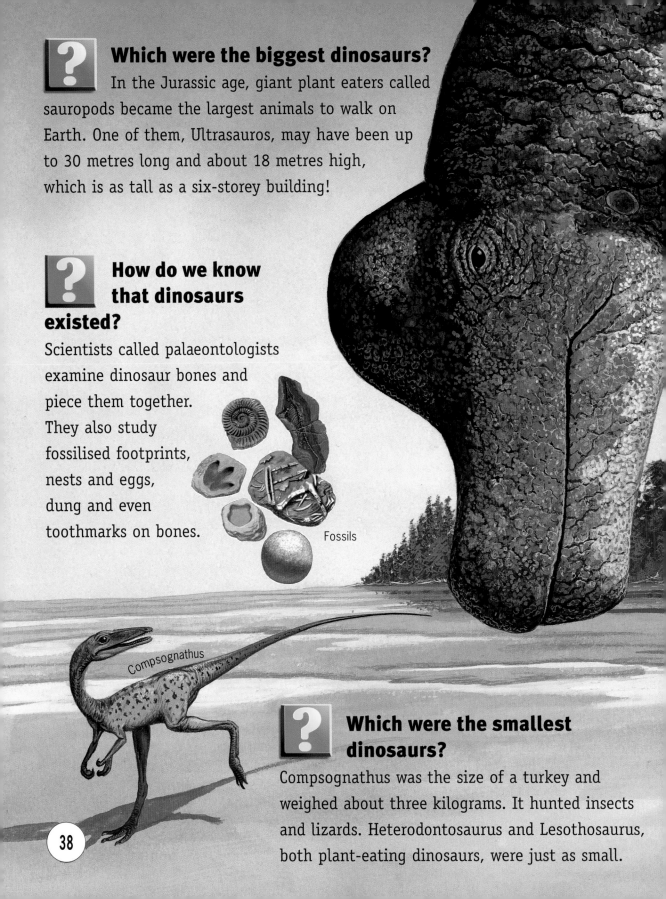

? Which were the biggest dinosaurs?

In the Jurassic age, giant plant eaters called sauropods became the largest animals to walk on Earth. One of them, Ultrasauros, may have been up to 30 metres long and about 18 metres high, which is as tall as a six-storey building!

? How do we know that dinosaurs existed?

Scientists called palaeontologists examine dinosaur bones and piece them together. They also study fossilised footprints, nests and eggs, dung and even toothmarks on bones.

Fossils

Compsognathus

? Which were the smallest dinosaurs?

Compsognathus was the size of a turkey and weighed about three kilograms. It hunted insects and lizards. Heterodontosaurus and Lesothosaurus, both plant-eating dinosaurs, were just as small.

Which were the heaviest dinosaurs?

Ultrasauros may have weighed as much as 50 tonnes, but scientists have recently found evidence of an even bigger dinosaur in Argentina. The gigantic Argentinosaurus may have weighed as much as 100 tonnes. Most sauropods were smaller, weighing between 30 and 80 tonnes.

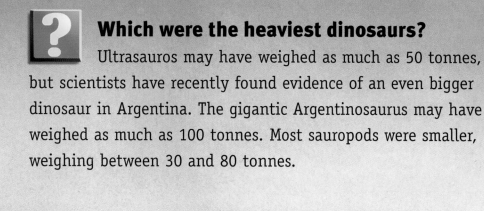

Ultrasauros

Amazing! The neck of Mamenchisaurus was 15 metres long, strengthened by a system of spines. It could not have been lifted very high. Mamenchisaurus probably fed on low-growing vegetation.

How do we know which dinosaurs ate meat, and which ate plants?

We can tell by looking at fossils of their teeth and claws. Meat eaters and plant eaters developed different special features, such as hands that could grasp and grinding or shearing teeth.

Plant-eater fossil

Meat-eater fossil

Yunnanosaurus

What were plant eaters' teeth like?

Yunnanosaurus had chisel-like teeth to cut up tough vegetation. Some sauropods had spoon-shaped teeth for cutting tough plants. Diplodocids had pencil-shaped teeth. They could strip branches bare in seconds by raking leaves through their teeth.

? What were meat eaters' teeth and claws like?

Meat eaters such as Allosaurus had long, curved, dagger-like teeth to kill and tear at prey. They had powerful jaws in their large heads and strong claws to grip their victims. Allosaurus could eat you up in two gulps!

Is it true?

Some dinosaurs ate stones.

Yes. Plant eaters swallowed stones called gastroliths, to help grind down tough plant food inside their stomachs. Gastroliths were up to ten cm across.

Allosaurus

 ## Amazing!

Carcharodontosaurus had a huge skull 1.6 metres across, with jaws full of teeth like a shark's. And yet some dinosaurs had no teeth at all! Gallimimus fed mainly on insects and tiny creatures it could swallow whole.

Tyrannosaurus rex

? Whose teeth were as long as knives?

Tyrannosaurus rex, one of the last dinosaurs, was also one of the largest and fiercest meat eaters ever to live on Earth. Its ferocious teeth were 15 cm long. It used them to strip away flesh while it held its prey down with its feet.

Tenontosaurus

Is it true?
Some dinosaurs were cannibals.

Yes. Two skeletons of Coelophysis have been found containing the bones of smaller Coelophysis. They had eaten the young animals as their last meal.

What would kick out at its prey?

Deinonychus had an enormous slashing claw on each foot. It probably hunted and killed in packs, attacking its prey with a flying leap.

Baryonyx

Deinonychus

Amazing!

Baryonyx had large, curved claws that may have been used for hooking fish out of water. Its jaw was very similar to the jaws of modern fish-eating crocodiles.

What had a 'terrible hand'?

Deinocheirus means 'terrible hand'. It had hands with long claws which must have been deadly, and arms three metres long. Compared to this, T. rex's arms were tiny!

? Were huge plant eaters ever attacked?

The sheer size of many of these gentle giants must have put off many predators. Some like Apatosaurus had long claws to defend themselves in case they were attacked. They would rear up on their back legs and slash out at their enemies.

Heterodontosaurus

Ceratosaurus

! Amazing! Plant
eaters like Heterodontosaurus had fangs which they may have used to bite attackers. It was a small but strong dinosaur, well able to defend itself against meat eaters.

Is it true?
Scientists can tell how quickly dinosaurs could travel.

YES. By looking at their skeletons and measuring the distance between fossilised footprints, scientists can measure how quickly or slowly a dinosaur moved.

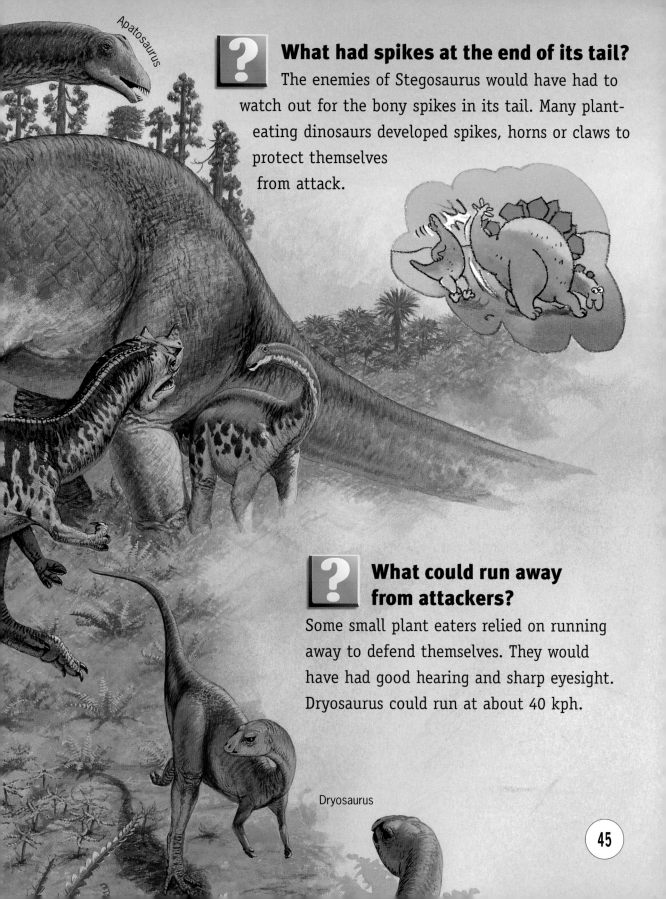

Apatosaurus

What had spikes at the end of its tail?

The enemies of Stegosaurus would have had to watch out for the bony spikes in its tail. Many plant-eating dinosaurs developed spikes, horns or claws to protect themselves from attack.

What could run away from attackers?

Some small plant eaters relied on running away to defend themselves. They would have had good hearing and sharp eyesight. Dryosaurus could run at about 40 kph.

Dryosaurus

45

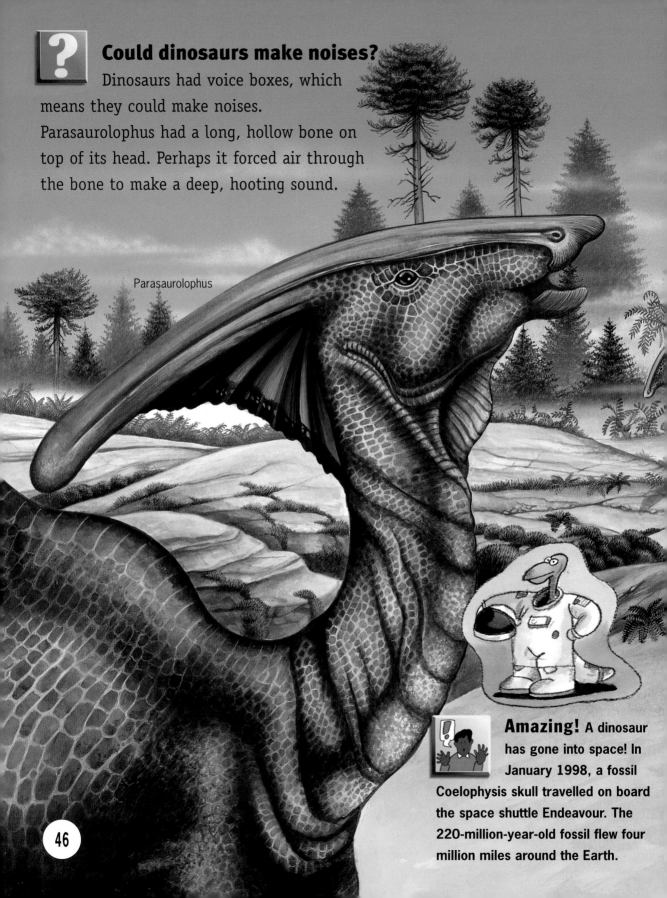

❓ Could dinosaurs make noises?

Dinosaurs had voice boxes, which means they could make noises. Parasaurolophus had a long, hollow bone on top of its head. Perhaps it forced air through the bone to make a deep, hooting sound.

Parasaurolophus

Amazing! A dinosaur has gone into space! In January 1998, a fossil Coelophysis skull travelled on board the space shuttle Endeavour. The 220-million-year-old fossil flew four million miles around the Earth.

46

Did dinosaurs care for their young?

Yes, some did. Maiasaura, whose name means 'good mother lizard', cared for its young. Parents looked after them until they were old enough to take care of themselves.

Maiasaura adult and young

Is it true?
Every animal on Earth died out with the dinosaurs.

NO. Lots of animals survived. Birds, mammals, amphibians, insects, small reptiles (lizards), fish, spiders, snails and crocodiles all lived.

 ## Why did dinosaurs die out?

Dinosaurs died out 65 million years ago. Many people think this was because a big meteorite (a space rock) hit the Earth. It sent dust into the air which blotted out the Sun. Dinosaurs died because they were too cold and hungry.

Meteorite hitting Earth

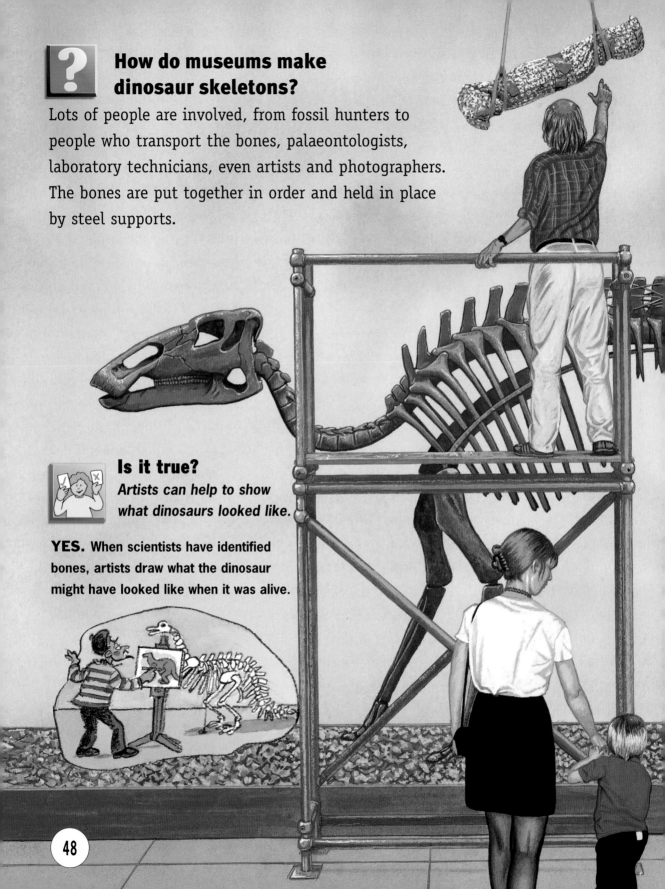

❓ How do museums make dinosaur skeletons?

Lots of people are involved, from fossil hunters to people who transport the bones, palaeontologists, laboratory technicians, even artists and photographers. The bones are put together in order and held in place by steel supports.

Is it true?
Artists can help to show what dinosaurs looked like.

YES. When scientists have identified bones, artists draw what the dinosaur might have looked like when it was alive.

Do museums use real bones?

No. Original fossils are too heavy and valuable. Instead scientists make copies from lightweight materials and keep the real bones safe.

STAFF ONLY

DINO DE TOUR

Amazing! Scientists think that they might have found a missing link between birds and dinosaurs. Sinosauropteryx was a true dinosaur, but it had a feathery covering, and its feet had sharp pointed claws, much like a chicken's.

Sinosauropteryx

CHAPTER THREE

EXPLORING EARTH

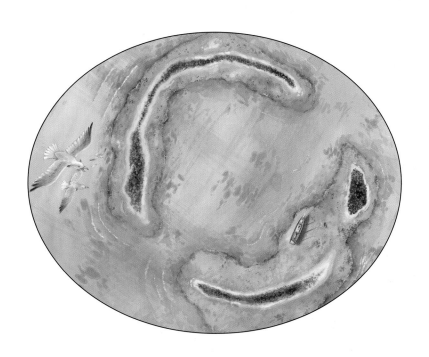

Earth

40,075 kilometres

? How big is the Earth?

The Earth is shaped like a gigantic ball, slightly squashed at the top and bottom. Around its middle, where it's fattest, it measures 40,075 kilometres. It would take you almost a year to walk right round the Earth, without a rest.

Interior of Earth

Inner mantle

Core

What's inside the Earth?

The Earth is made up of layers of rock and metal. We live on the hard, rocky surface, called the crust. Below, the layers are so hot that they've melted and turned runny. The centre of the Earth is a ball of almost solid metal.

Crust and atmosphere

Lithosphere

Outer mantle

Amazing!

People used to think the Earth was flat. If they sailed too far in one direction, they thought they'd fall off the edge!

What are the continents?

The Earth's rocky crust is cracked into several gigantic pieces and lots of smaller chunks. The large pieces contain the seven continents - Africa, Antarctica, Asia, Australasia, Europe, North America and South America. Which of the continents do you live on?

Earth's main continental plates

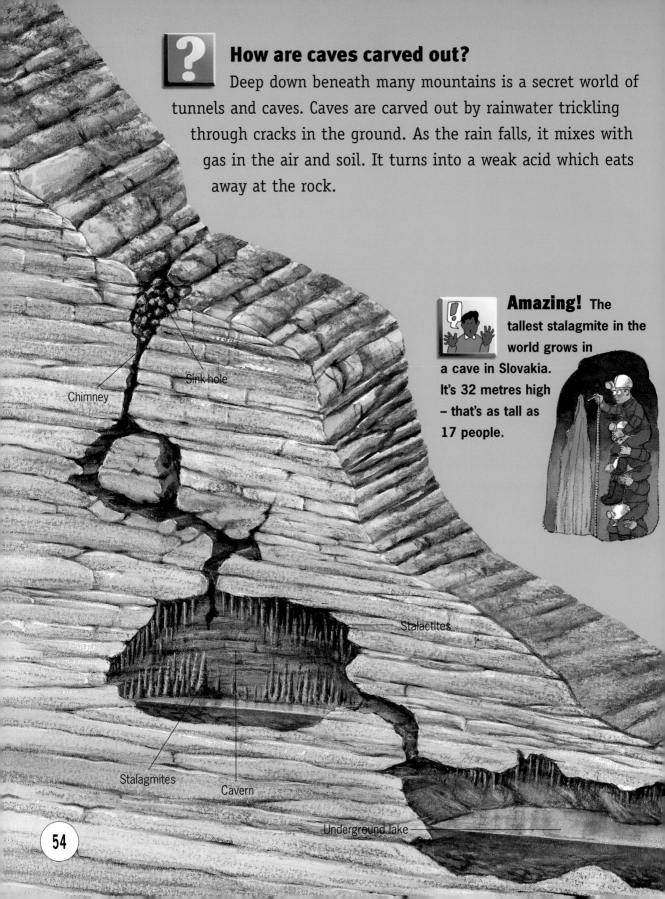

? How are caves carved out?

Deep down beneath many mountains is a secret world of tunnels and caves. Caves are carved out by rainwater trickling through cracks in the ground. As the rain falls, it mixes with gas in the air and soil. It turns into a weak acid which eats away at the rock.

Amazing! The tallest stalagmite in the world grows in a cave in Slovakia. It's 32 metres high – that's as tall as 17 people.

Chimney

Sink-hole

Stalactites

Stalagmites

Cavern

Underground lake

Mammoth Caves, Kentucky, USA

 Where are the longest caves?

The Mammoth Caves in Kentucky are the longest caves on Earth. They stretch for 560 kilometres. The biggest single cave is the Sarawak Chamber in Malaysia. Its floor is the size of 30 soccer pitches.

Prehistoric cave art

 Which caves are art galleries?

Thousands of years ago, prehistoric people sheltered in caves, and painted pictures on the walls. The best art gallery is in the Lascaux Caves in France. The walls are covered with hundreds of animals, including bison and mammoths.

Limestone cave system

 Is it true?
Potholers are people who explore caves.

YES. Even though it's wet, cold and dark underground. The deepest a potholer has ever been is 1,508 metres in a cave in Russia.

How are mountains built?

Some mountains are built when two pieces of the Earth's crust bump or crash into each other. The rock in between is pushed up into giant fold mountains. Other mountains are made when huge blocks of rocks are squeezed up.

Himalayas

Himalayan mountain range

Mountains are formed as rocks are squeezed upward by the force of India pushing against Asia

Over millions of years, the island of India moved towards the continent of Asia, until eventually they met

Amazing! The first people to climb to the top of Mt Everest were Sherpa Tenzing Norgay and Edmund Hillary in 1953.

? Why are mountains shrinking?

It takes millions of years for mountains to grow. But many are shrinking every day. Mountains are being worn away by wind, frost and ice, which attack the peaks and break off chips of rock.

Shrinking mountain

? Where are the highest mountains?

The highest mountains in the world are the Himalayas in Asia. This massive mountain range has 12 of the world's 14 highest peaks, including Mt Everest. At 8,848 metres, it's the highest mountain on Earth.

 Is it true?
The higher up a mountain you go, the hotter it gets.

NO. The higher you go, the colder it gets. That's why the tops of some peaks are capped in snow – and why many mountain animals have warm, winter coats.

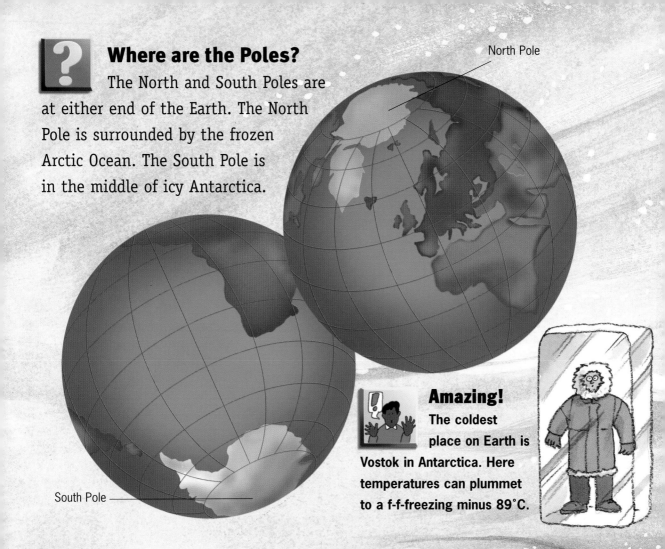

? Where are the Poles?

The North and South Poles are at either end of the Earth. The North Pole is surrounded by the frozen Arctic Ocean. The South Pole is in the middle of icy Antarctica.

North Pole

South Pole

Amazing!

The coldest place on Earth is Vostok in Antarctica. Here temperatures can plummet to a f-f-freezing minus 89°C.

? Why are the Poles cold?

The Poles are the coldest places on Earth. They're battered by blizzards and covered in ice and snow. The Poles are cold because the Sun's rays hit them at a slant, so they're spread out and very weak.

Sun's rays
Pole

Equator

58

NO. Penguins only live around the South Pole. But you might bump into a polar bear at the North Pole.

Who reached the South Pole first?

The first person to reach the South Pole was Norwegian explorer Roald Amundsen in December 1911. He beat the British team of Captain Scott by about a month. Exhausted and suffering from frostbite, Scott died on the way home.

Captain Scott in the Antarctic

Amazing! In 1912, the luxury liner, Titanic, hit an iceberg and sank in the North Atlantic. It was on its maiden (first) voyage from Southampton to New York.

What are icebergs?

Icebergs are giant chunks of ice that break off the ends of glaciers and drift out to sea. Only about a tenth of an iceberg shows above water. The rest is hidden under the sea. This makes them very dangerous to passing ships and boats.

Iceberg seen from underwater

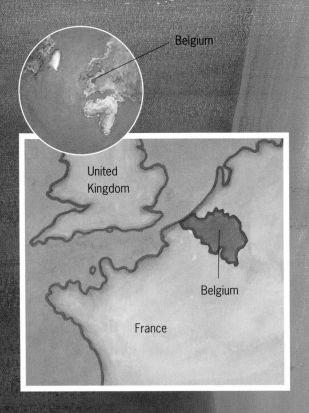

Belgium

United Kingdom

Belgium

France

Which was the biggest iceberg?

The biggest iceberg ever was seen near Antarctica. It was about the size of Belgium! The tallest iceberg was more than half as high as the Eiffel Tower in Paris.

Is it true?

Baby icebergs are called calves.

YES. A baby iceberg breaking off a glacier is called 'calving'. Even smaller icebergs are called 'bergy bits'.

? Which is the longest glacier?

Glaciers are enormous rivers of ice that flow slowly down a mountainside. The Lambert-Fisher Glacier in Antarctica is over 600 kilometres long. It's the longest glacier in the world. About a tenth of the Earth is covered in icy glaciers.

Glacier

Why does the sea flow in and out?

Twice a day, the sea washes on to the shore at high tide. Then it flows back out again at low tide. The tides are caused by the Moon and Sun pulling the sea into giant bulges on either side of the Earth.

Amazing!

If all the coasts were straightened out, they'd stretch round the Earth 13 times. At 90,000 kilometres, Canada has the longest coast.

Cliffs being worn down to make sand

62

Why are beaches sandy?

Sand is made from tiny fragments of rock and shells, crushed up by the wind and water. Sand is usually yellow or white. But some sand is black because it contains volcanic rock or coal.

Sandy beach

How are cliffs carved out?

Along the coast, the rocks are worn away by the force of the waves. As the waves crash against the shore, they carve out cliffs, caves and high arches. Sometimes an arch collapses, leaving a stack, or pillar, of rock.

Stack

Features of chalk cliffs

Arch

Headland

Is it true?

White horses swim in the sea.

YES. But they're not real horses. They're the white, foamy tops of the waves as they gallop towards the shore.

? How big is the sea?

The sea is absolutely huge! Salty sea water covers about two-thirds of our planet so there's far more sea than land. The sea lies in five oceans – the Pacific, Atlantic, Indian, Arctic and Southern Oceans.

Amazing! The first person to set sail around the world was Ferdinand Magellan. He set off from Spain in 1519. Magellan died but one of his ships made it back three years later.

Arctic Ocean

Atlantic Ocean

Southern Ocean

Which is the biggest ocean?

By far the biggest ocean is the vast Pacific. It alone covers a third of the Earth. At its widest point, between Panama and Malaysia, it stretches almost halfway around the world.

Malaysia

Pacific Ocean

an Ocean

Panama

Southern Ocean

Is it true?
The Arctic is the warmest ocean.

NO. The Arctic's the coldest ocean of all. For most of the year, it's covered in ice.

Why is the sea salty?

The sea's salty taste comes from ordinary salt. It's the same stuff you sprinkle on your food. The rain washes the salt out of rocks on land, then rivers carry it into the sea. The people in the picture are collecting salt left after sea water dries.

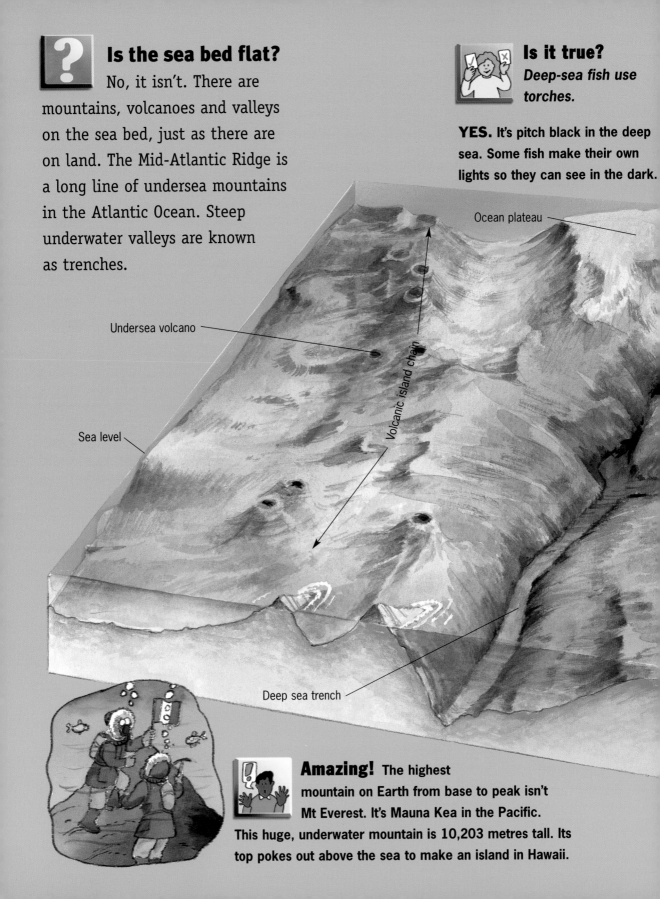

Is the sea bed flat?

No, it isn't. There are mountains, volcanoes and valleys on the sea bed, just as there are on land. The Mid-Atlantic Ridge is a long line of undersea mountains in the Atlantic Ocean. Steep underwater valleys are known as trenches.

Ocean plateau

Undersea volcano

Sea level

Volcanic island chain

Deep sea trench

Amazing! The highest mountain on Earth from base to peak isn't Mt Everest. It's Mauna Kea in the Pacific. This huge, underwater mountain is 10,203 metres tall. Its top pokes out above the sea to make an island in Hawaii.

? Who builds coral reefs?

Huge coral reefs are built by tiny sea creatures called polyps. The polyps build hard, stony cases around their soft bodies. When they die, the cases are left behind. Millions and millions make a coral reef.

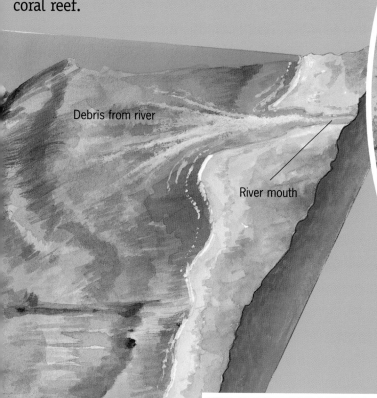

Debris from river

River mouth

Continental shelf

Coral reef

Deep-sea submersible

? Who dived the deepest?

In 1960, two scientists dived nearly 11 kilometres into the Marianas Trench in the Pacific Ocean. This is the deepest dive ever made. They travelled in a small submersible called Trieste. It took almost five hours to reach the bottom.

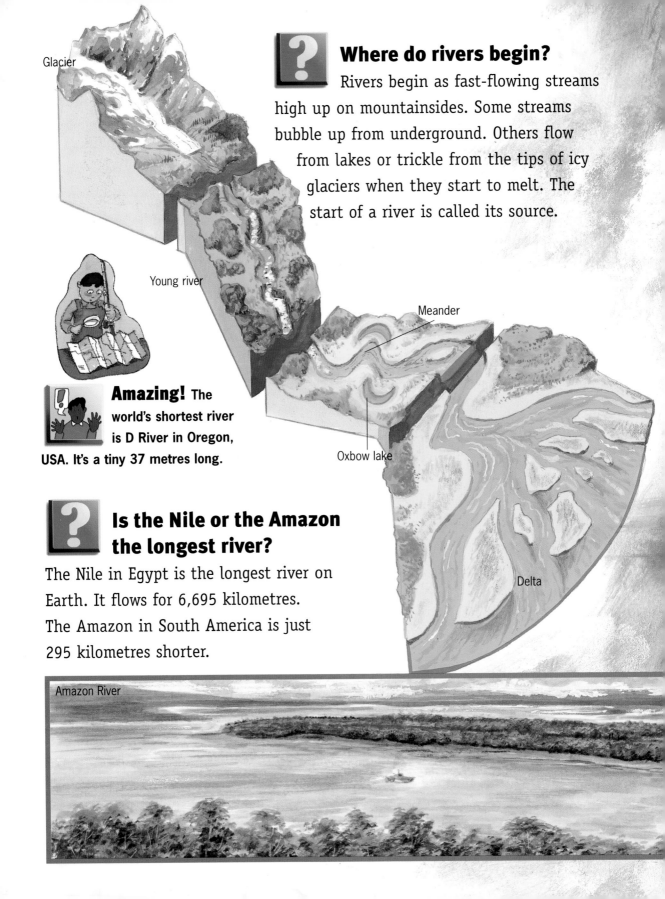

Glacier

Where do rivers begin?

Rivers begin as fast-flowing streams high up on mountainsides. Some streams bubble up from underground. Others flow from lakes or trickle from the tips of icy glaciers when they start to melt. The start of a river is called its source.

Young river

Meander

Amazing! The world's shortest river is D River in Oregon, USA. It's a tiny 37 metres long.

Oxbow lake

Is the Nile or the Amazon the longest river?

The Nile in Egypt is the longest river on Earth. It flows for 6,695 kilometres. The Amazon in South America is just 295 kilometres shorter.

Delta

Amazon River

Angel Falls

❓ How high are waterfalls?

The highest waterfall in the world is Angel Falls in Venezuela. It plunges 979 metres down the side of a mountain. Angel Falls are 20 times higher than the famous Niagara Falls in North America.

Is it true?
Rivers flow into the sea.

YES. Most rivers flow into the sea at their deltas. But some rivers flow into lakes and a few flow into deserts.

69

? Which lake is the biggest?

The biggest freshwater lake on Earth is Lake Superior in North America. It covers 82,350 square kilometres. That's almost as big as Austria. Lake Superior is one of five huge lakes called the Great Lakes.

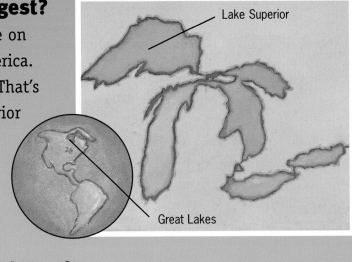

Lake Superior

Great Lakes

✓✗ Is it true?

There's a monster in Loch Ness.

MAYBE. Some people say Nessie is a type of prehistoric reptile that lives in the lake. Others say this is nonsense. What do you think?

Volcanic lake

Oxbow lake

Amazing! The Dead Sea in the Middle East is so salty that you can float on the surface. No fish can live in it.

Lake Titicaca

❓ Where is the highest lake?

Lake Titicaca in South America is the highest lake on which boats can sail. It's 3,810 metres up in the Andes Mountains. People who live around the lake build boats from lake reeds.

Tarn

Glacial lake

River basin lake

❓ How are lakes made?

Some lakes formed long ago, in hollows scraped out by ice. These filled with water as the ice melted. Some lakes form in the tops of volcanoes or when a river cuts through a bend.

71

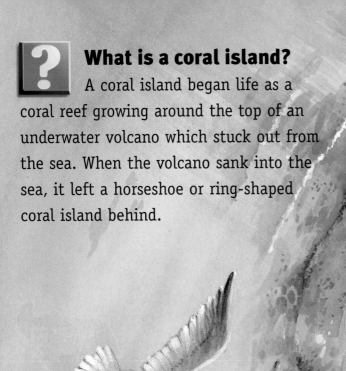

❓ What is a coral island?

A coral island began life as a coral reef growing around the top of an underwater volcano which stuck out from the sea. When the volcano sank into the sea, it left a horseshoe or ring-shaped coral island behind.

Amazing!
If you lived on the island of Tristan da Cunha in the South Atlantic, your nearest neighbours would be almost 2,500 kilometres away.

❓ Where is the biggest island?

An island is a chunk of land with water all around it. The biggest island is Greenland, in the icy Arctic Ocean. It measures more than 2 million square kilometres. Australia is bigger than that, but it usually counts as a continent.

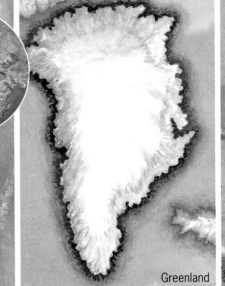

Greenland

Which country has most islands?

The country of Indonesia in South East Asia is made up of more than 13,000 islands. But many of the islands are tiny and people only live on about 1,500 of them.

Coral island

Central lagoon

Coral island seen from above

Reef

Is it true?
New islands keep being made.

YES. In 1963, a new island, called Surtsey, burst out of the sea near Iceland when an undersea volcano erupted.

? Why are deserts dry?

Deserts are the driest places on Earth. In some deserts it doesn't rain for years at a time. In others, it never rains at all. Some deserts are also scorching hot. In the daytime, the sand's hot enough to fry an egg on.

 Amazing! The Sahara Desert is the biggest, sandiest desert in the world. It covers about a third of Africa.

Sandy desert seen from above

? Can sand dunes move?

Strong winds blowing across the desert pile the sand up into giant heaps, or dunes. The biggest stand 200 metres tall. The dunes creep forward every year and can bury whole desert villages.

Sand dunes covering a town

74

Mesa

Butte

Sand dunes

Desert landscapes

Salt lake

Dried salt flat

Rocky desert

Volcanic desert

? Are all deserts sandy?

No, they're not. Only about a quarter of all deserts are sandy. Most deserts are rocky or covered in gravel and stones. Some deserts have high mountains or strange-shaped rocks towering up from the ground.

Is it true?
Mushrooms grow in the desert.

YES. Well, mushroom-shaped rocks. They're carved into shape by sand blown by the wind, like a giant piece of sandpaper.

? Why are rainforests so wet?

Because it rains almost every single day! Late most afternoons, the sky goes black and there's a heavy thunderstorm. Rainforests grow along the equator where it's hot and sticky all year round. It's the perfect weather for plants to grow.

Rainforest

Coniferous forest

Where do the biggest forests grow?

The biggest forests in the world stretch for thousands of kilometres across the north of Europe and Asia. The trees that grow here are conifers. They're trees with needle-like leaves and cones.

Is it true?
The paper we use comes from forests.

YES. You could make more than 1,500 copies of this book from a single conifer tree.

Amazing!
The biggest rainforest grows in South America along the banks of the River Amazon. It's home to millions of plants and animals.

Rainforest layers

Emergent layer

Canopy layer

Understorey

Ground layer

How do rainforests grow?

Rainforests grow in layers depending on the height of the trees. The tallest trees poke out above the forest. Below them is a thick roof of tree-tops called the canopy. Next comes a layer of shorter trees, herbs and shrubs.

African savannah (grassland)

? What are grasslands?

Grasslands are huge plains of grass, trees and bushes. They grow in warm, dry places where there's too little rain for forests to grow, but enough rain to stop the land turning into a desert.

South American gauchos farming on grassland

❓ Why did a grassland turn to dust?

In the 1930s, farmers in the south-west USA ploughed up the grasslands to grow wheat. But a terrible drought turned the soil to dry, useless dust which blew away in the wind. This was called a dustbowl.

Dustbowl

❗ Amazing!
Grassland animals eat different bits of the grass to avoid competition – zebras eat the tops, wildebeest eat the stems.

❓ What are grasslands used for?

People use grasslands for grazing animals such as cattle which are raised for their meat. They also grow crops such as wheat and barley in gigantic fields. One wheat field in Canada was the size of 20,000 soccer pitches.

Is it true?
Rice is a type of grass.

YES. Rice is a cereal plant, which belongs to the grass family. The grains of rice come from the flower-heads. Rice grows in flooded fields in South East Asia.

CHAPTER FOUR

VIOLENT EARTH

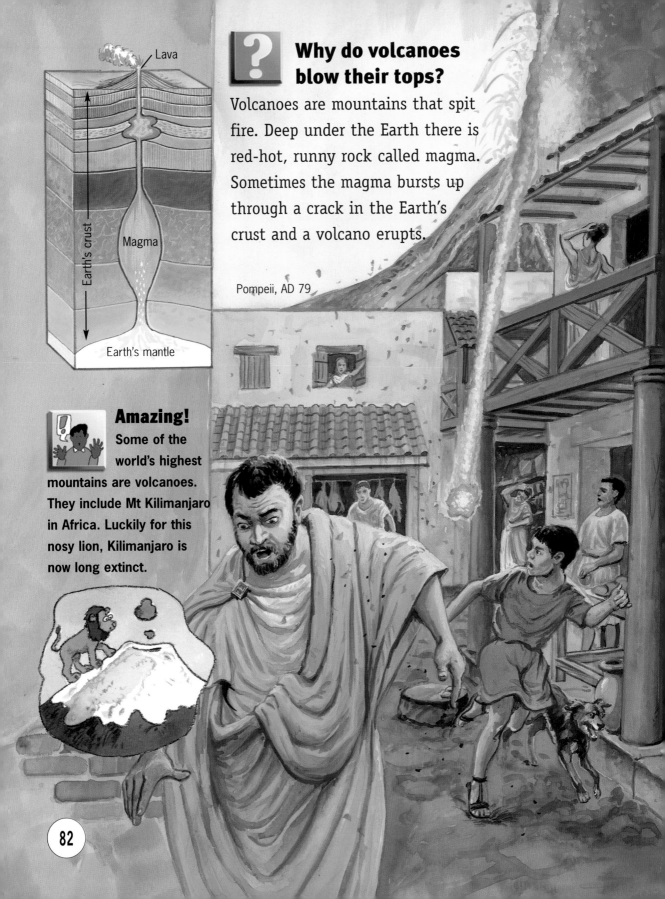

Lava

Earth's crust

Magma

Earth's mantle

? Why do volcanoes blow their tops?

Volcanoes are mountains that spit fire. Deep under the Earth there is red-hot, runny rock called magma. Sometimes the magma bursts up through a crack in the Earth's crust and a volcano erupts.

Pompeii, AD 79

! Amazing!

Some of the world's highest mountains are volcanoes. They include Mt Kilimanjaro in Africa. Luckily for this nosy lion, Kilimanjaro is now long extinct.

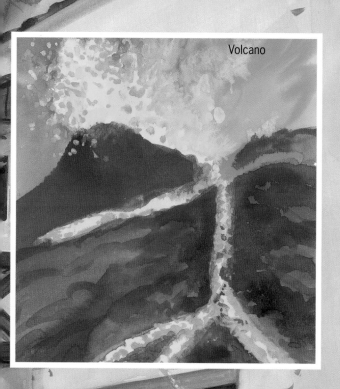

Volcano

What is lava?

Once magma has erupted from a volcano, it is called lava. Some lava is thick and lumpy. Some is thin and runny. In the air, it cools and turns into hard, black rock.

Is it true?

Volcanic ash can flow as fast as a train.

YES. Clouds of gas and ash can flow across the ground at over 160 kph!

What happened to Pompeii?

In AD 79, Mt Vesuvius in Italy blew its top in a massive explosion. The nearby city of Pompeii was buried under a huge cloud of hot ash and rock. Thousands of people were suffocated. Others fled for their lives.

Mt St Helen's, USA was a dormant volcano that erupted

? How long do volcanoes sleep for?

Hundreds or even thousands of years. A sleeping volcano is called dormant, but it can wake up at any minute. A volcano that still erupts is called active. An extinct volcano is one that is never likely to erupt again.

Geyser in Yellowstone Park, USA

Amazing! The most active volcano on Earth is Kilauea in Hawaii. It has erupted non-stop for almost 20 years! All that lava means the island of Hawaii is getting bigger every day.

? Why do people live near volcanoes?

Despite the danger, many people all over the world live near volcanoes. The ash that explodes out of a volcano makes the soil very rich for growing crops. People also use volcanic rock for building.

Is it true?
You only get volcanoes on land.

NO. There are hundreds of volcanoes on land and many more under the sea. Some poke out above the surface to form islands, such as Hawaii.

Town covered in ash after eruption of Mt Pinatubo, Philippines

? Why do geysers gush?

Geysers are giant jets of scalding water and steam. They happen in places with lots of volcanoes. The red-hot rocks underground heat water far below the surface until it's so hot it shoots through a crack.

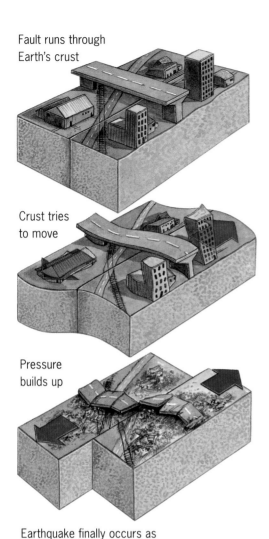

Fault runs through Earth's crust

Crust tries to move

Pressure builds up

Earthquake finally occurs as pieces move apart with a jerk

What makes the Earth shake?

The Earth's surface is cracked into enormous pieces which drift on the red-hot, runny rock below. Sometimes two pieces push and shove each other, making the Earth shake.

Kobe earthquake, Japan, 1995

How much damage do earthquakes cause?

Big earthquakes do lots of damage. Huge cracks open up in the ground. Houses, roads and bridges shake and fall down. In the worst earthquakes, many people are killed and injured by buildings that collapse on top of them.

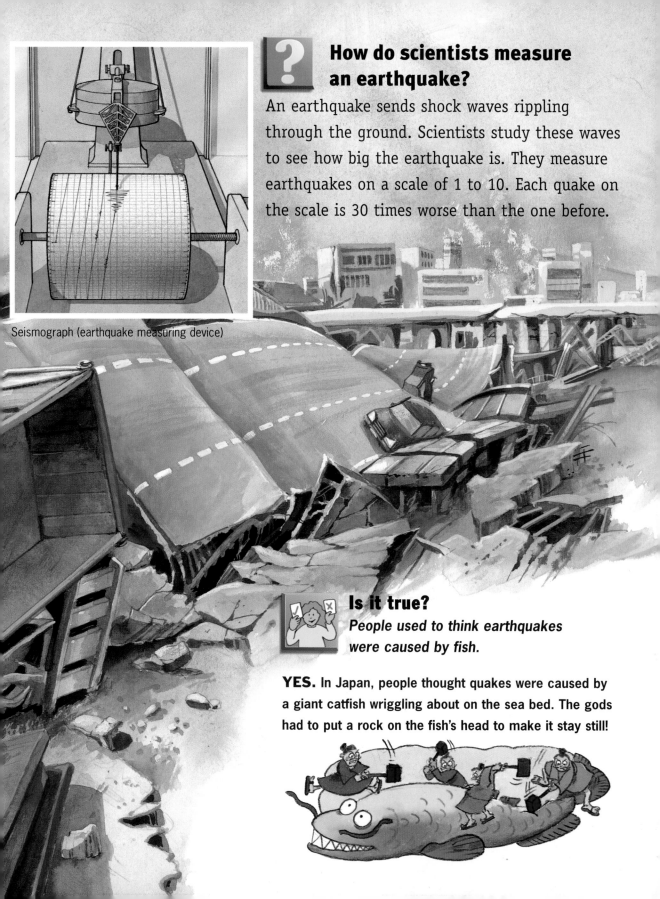

Seismograph (earthquake measuring device)

? How do scientists measure an earthquake?

An earthquake sends shock waves rippling through the ground. Scientists study these waves to see how big the earthquake is. They measure earthquakes on a scale of 1 to 10. Each quake on the scale is 30 times worse than the one before.

Is it true?

People used to think earthquakes were caused by fish.

YES. In Japan, people thought quakes were caused by a giant catfish wriggling about on the sea bed. The gods had to put a rock on the fish's head to make it stay still!

What is a tsunami?

Tsunamis are gigantic waves which can be 30 metres high and 200 kilometres long. The word tsunami means 'harbour wave' in Japanese because of the way the waves crash into the harbour. They are also called tidal waves.

Is it true?

The biggest tsunami was as tall as the Statue of Liberty.

YES. This colossal wave was 85 metres high, almost as tall as the Statue of Liberty. It swept past Japan in 1971.

Amazing!

A tsunami can travel across the sea at high speed. Some race along at 900 kph. That's as fast as a jet plane. The deeper the water, the faster they flow.

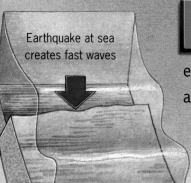

Earthquake at sea creates fast waves

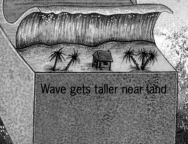

Wave gets taller near land

How do tsunamis start?

Tsunamis are triggered off by volcanoes or earthquakes under the sea. At first, the waves are low as they speed across the sea. As they reach land, the water piles up into a massive wave which crashes down on to the shore.

Tsunamis can leave boats stranded inland

What happens when a tsunami hits land?

When a tsunami hits land, watch out! It smashes down on to the shore, washing houses, people and boats away. A tsunami can sweep a boat into the air and dump it far away.

89

? How do floods happen?

Many floods happen when it rains very heavily and rivers overflow. They burst their banks and flood the land all around. You also get floods in stormy weather when high tides or gigantic waves sweep on to the shore.

Amazing! The Thames Barrier was finished in 1984 to stop the River Thames flooding and drowning London. Ten huge steel gates swing up to make a massive dam.

Flash flood of Ouvèze River, France

What are flash floods?

Flash floods are floods which happen very suddenly, with no warning. Sometimes there isn't time to evacuate buildings in the flood's path. Flash floods can happen in the desert too, during a rare downpour of rain.

River Nile in flood

Are some floods useful?

Yes, they are. The River Nile in Egypt used to flood every year, leaving rich mud on the fields. The mud made the soil ideal for farmers to grow bumper crops. The Nile doesn't flood any more because a large dam was built to store its water.

Is it true?

Floods can wash whole buildings away.

YES. In 1955, a flood in the USA washed a four-storey wooden hotel clean away. Imagine how surprised the guests were when they looked out of their windows!

The Mississippi River, USA, flooded 80,000 square kilometres, in 1993

When do thunderstorms happen?

Thunderstorms usually happen on a hot, summer's day when the air is warm and sticky. Watch out for huge, dark, tall thunderclouds gathering in the sky. They're a sure sign a storm's brewing. Time to head indoors!

What makes thunder rumble?

Lightning is incredibly hot, about five times hotter than the Sun's surface. As it streaks through the sky, it heats the air so quickly that it makes a loud booming sound. This is the sound of thunder.

❓ Where do thunderstorms begin?

Thunder starts in cumulonimbus clouds. They turn the sky purply black and blue. Some of these clouds are massive. The tallest can grow 18 kilometres high. That's more than twice the height of Mt Everest.

Is it true?
Lightning happens before thunder.

NO. They happen at exactly the same time. But you see lightning before you hear thunder because light travels more quickly than sound.

Cumulonimbus thundercloud

Amazing! The Vikings believed that thunder was caused by the bad-tempered god, Thor, hurling his hammer across the sky.

What makes lightning flash?

Inside a thundercloud, strong winds hurl droplets of water around. They bump and bash into each other. This makes the cloud crackle with static electricity which builds up and suddenly streaks through the sky as lightning. Lightning can flash inside clouds or from cloud to ground.

Amazing!

Park ranger, Roy C. Sullivan, was struck by lightning a record seven times. He suffered burns, singed hair and eyebrows, and he even lost his toenails!

Empire State Building, New York City, during thunderstorm

Does lightning ever strike twice?

Yes, it does. The Empire State Building is struck about 500 times a year! Many tall buildings, such as churches and skyscrapers, have lightning conductors to carry the electricity of the lightning safely away.

There are many stories of ball lightning entering houses

? What is ball lightning?

Lightning comes in different shapes, such as forked, sheet and ribbon lightning. Ball lightning looks like a ball of fire. People have seen balls of lightning float into their house, then explode with a bang.

Is it true?

Lightning takes the slowest path to the ground.

NO. It takes the quickest. That's why you should never shelter under a tall tree during a storm. If the lightning strikes the tree, you might get fried.

Where do avalanches strike?

Avalanches strike on snow-covered mountainsides. A huge slab of snow and ice suddenly breaks loose and crashes downhill. Avalanches can slide at speeds of up to 320 kph, as fast as a racing car, as hundreds of tonnes of snow hurtle down the slope.

Sniffer dogs search for buried victims

Can people survive avalanches?

Avalanches are deadly. They can bury people, cars and whole villages in their path. Victims suffocate under the snow unless they're rescued quickly. Rescue teams use specially trained dogs to sniff survivors out.

Amazing! In World War I, soldiers fighting each other in the Alps used avalanches as weapons. They fired guns at the mountainsides to set off killer avalanches.

Is it true?

Yodelling can set off an avalanche.

YES. In some Swiss mountain villages yodelling is banned in spring in case it sets an avalanche off. You're not allowed to shout or sing loudly either, in case the vibrations of sound waves in the air shake and loosen the snow, to start an avalanche.

? What sets off an avalanche?

If the snow gets too heavy, it can suddenly start to slip and slide. But other things can trigger an avalanche. A skier, or even a car door being slammed, can set the snow sliding.

Layers of snow and ice build up on mountainside

Weight of snow creates cracks, and a large chunk slips away

97

Why are blizzards dangerous?

A blizzard is a snowstorm. Strong winds blow the snow into drifts and it can be difficult to see. A blizzard can bring a busy city to a standstill. People and traffic can't move about, and schools and offices have to be closed.

Amazing! You don't only get snow in cold places. In 1981, snow fell in the Kalahari Desert in Africa for the first time in living memory. The temperature dropped to a chilly minus 5°C.

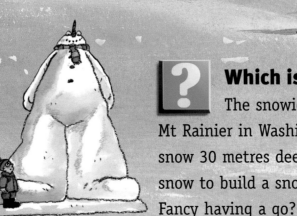

Which is the snowiest place?

The snowiest place in the world is Mt Rainier in Washington, USA. In one year, snow 30 metres deep fell there. That's enough snow to build a snowman as tall as 17 people. Fancy having a go?

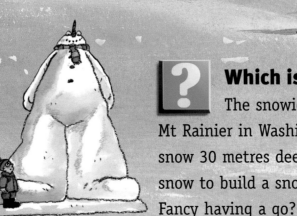

98

What is a hailstone made from?

A hailstone is a small ball of ice that starts life in a thundercloud. Inside the cloud, a chip of ice is tossed up and down many times. It gets coated in layers of ice, just like the layers of an onion.

Cutaway of a hailstone, showing the layers of ice

Build-up of a hailstone within a thundercloud

Is it true?
The biggest hailstone was the size of a peach.

NO. It was bigger than that! Hailstones are usually the size of peas but the biggest was the size of a watermelon. It fell in Kansas, USA, in 1970.

Record-breaking hailstone

❓ What are hurricanes?

Hurricanes are giant storms that begin over warm tropical seas. They are like huge spinning wheels of wind, rain and clouds. They sweep across the sea, then begin to die down when they reach land.

Cutaway of a hurricane

Eye

Rain

Is it true?
Hurricanes have names.

YES. Hurricanes are given names from an alphabetical list. A new list is made every year. The names of the worst hurricanes, like Andrew or Carol, are never used again.

Andrew

Carol

How big are hurricanes?

Hurricanes can be enormous. Some measure 3,000 kilometres across and even the smallest are about half the size of Britain. Winds inside a hurricane can blow at over 300 kph.

Hurricanes can even pick up and dump aeroplanes

Amazing!

If you could collect the energy inside a hurricane for one day and turn it into electricity, it would run the whole USA for six months.

An Atlantic hurricane hits the island of Antigua

Eye of hurricane seen from space

Do hurricanes have eyes?

Yes, they do. The eye is a patch of calm, clear weather in the hurricane's centre. As the eye passes over land, there's a break in the storm for an hour or so. Then it begins again.

? What makes a tornado twist?

A tornado is a fierce, twisting wind which hangs from a thundercloud. It starts when wind inside the cloud starts to spin very quickly. A twisty tornado speeds across the ground, sucking up everything in its way.

Storm chasers observing a tornado in Kansas, USA

Amazing! Some people track tornadoes for fun. They drive as close to the twister as they dare, then take video films and photographs. It's a very dangerous hobby!

A tornado leaving a trail of damage

 ## Is it true?

Tornadoes can pick up trains.

YES. In 1931, a tornado in Minnesota, USA, picked a train right off its tracks and dumped it in a ditch. Tornadoes often pick up cars and cows!

 ## How quickly do tornadoes travel?

Most tornadoes travel at about 30 kph, but some are much speedier movers. They race along the ground as quickly as a car. What's more, the wind inside a tornado can blow at an amazing 480 kph.

Do tornadoes happen at sea?

Yes, they're called waterspouts. These giant twists of water can be over 1.5 kilometres tall. In the past, sailors thought waterspouts were sea monsters!

Waterspouts suck up tonnes of water from the sea

Firefighting plane

? How do wildfires start?

They destroy huge patches of forest, and spread very quickly, especially in dry weather. Lightning starts hundreds of wildfires a year. But most fires are started intentionally by people to clear space for farms and fields. These fires can quickly get out of control.

Is it true?
Some trees have fireproof bark.

YES. Many trees die in forest fires because their wood easily catches fire. But some trees have special bark which protects the wood inside from the flames.

? How do people fight wildfires?

Fighting a wildfire is difficult and dangerous. Special planes fly overhead spraying the forest with millions of litres of water. Firefighters on the ground try to hold back the fire with water and beaters.

Firefighters battle a large wildfire

? What is a heatwave?

A heatwave is very hot weather which lasts much longer than usual. The scorching heat can kill people, animals and crops. It also dries up reservoirs, and melts the surface of roads.

Duststorm during the Midwest USA heatwave, 1937

 Amazing! It can take hundreds of years for a forest to grow again after a fire. But sometimes fires can be good for forests. They clear space for new plants to grow.

Landslide

❓ What makes the land slide?

A landslide is a huge fall of soil or mud which suddenly breaks off a cliff or mountainside and slides downhill. Some landslides are caused by volcanoes, heavy rain, or earthquakes, which make the ground shake and slip.

❓ Where was the worst mudslide?

The worst mudslide happened in Colombia in South America. In 1985, a volcano erupted and melted masses of snow and ice, turning the soil to mud. The mud poured downhill at top speed and buried a whole town.

Mudslide survivors are rescued by helicopter in Armero, Colombia

? Why do cliffs collapse?

As the waves crash against a cliff, they wear the bottom of the cliff away. If the cliff becomes too top-heavy, it collapses into the sea. Along the east coast of England, whole cliff-top villages have toppled into the sea.

Cliff collapsing into the sea

Amazing! Mudslides can slide at high speeds of up to 110 kph. They can slither along for as much as 100 kilometres before coming to a stop.

107

El Niño is represented by the red areas along the centre of the Earth

? What is El Niño?

El Niño is a warm band of water which flows in the sea along the coast of South America. Scientists blame El Niño for changing the weather, by causing more storms, floods, droughts and tornadoes every few years.

Is it true?
It can rain cats and dogs.

NO. But you can get showers of fish, frogs, flowers, coal, nuts and even maggots! Scientists think the wind scoops them up, then they fall again in the rain.

What are monsoons?

Monsoons are winds which bring heavy rain to tropical places such as India and South East Asia, during the summer months. Farmers rely on this rain to water their crops, because during the cooler months, there might be little or no rainfall.

Amazing! A turtle once fell in a hailstone in the USA. It had somehow been sucked up into a thundercloud and covered in layers of ice.

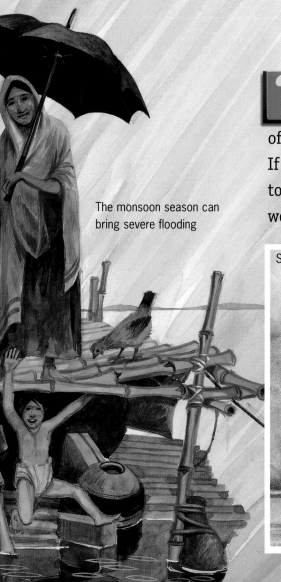

The monsoon season can bring severe flooding

What is a sandstorm?

A sandstorm is a thick, choking cloud of sand whipped up by the wind in the desert. If you get caught in a sandstorm the best thing to do is cover your nose and mouth. Then you won't breathe the choking sand in.

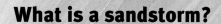

Sandstorm in Africa

CHAPTER FIVE

OUR
EARTH

Is Earth a healthy planet?

Look at Earth from space and you see a mainly blue, watery planet with swirling white clouds. All looks well, but get closer, and you see a different picture. Parts of Earth are unhealthy – and all because of the way we live.

Earth seen from space

Does Earth need looking after?

Earth is our only home – we can't live on other planets. We need to look after it to make sure it stays a beautiful, healthy place. If we don't care for the Earth now, we will spoil it for the people of the future.

? Can I help care for the Earth?

There are many things you can do in your everyday life to care for the Earth. This book tells you about some of them. Just think, if everyone did the same as you, Earth would be a better place to live.

Our Solar System has nine planets which orbit the Sun

 Is it true?
There is no other planet like Earth.

YES. There is only one Earth. It is special – it is the only planet known to have life on it. Perhaps one day life will be found on another planet, too.

Amazing! There has been life on Earth for approximately 3.5 billion years.

Is Earth's climate changing?

Earth's climate is slowly getting warmer. Scientists who study the climate have found that it is a little warmer now than it was 100 years ago. You may not notice the difference, but plants and animals do.

Climate study in the Antarctic

Is it true?

Trees reduce carbon dioxide in the atmosphere.

YES. Tree leaves take harmful carbon dioxide from the atmosphere and give out oxygen. We breathe the oxygen they make.

Cars and factories burn 'fossil fuels' which produce harmful 'greenhouse gases'

? Why is the temperature rising?

It's getting warmer because of what the Earth's 6 billion people are doing. Because of the way we lead our lives, we are changing the Earth's climate. We are making the planet grow warmer.

 Amazing! There is far more carbon dioxide in the atmosphere than there was 200 years ago. This is mainly why it's warmer today than it was in the past.

? How are we making the temperature rise?

By burning 'fossil fuels' – coal, oil and natural gas – we are putting 'greenhouse gases', such as carbon dioxide, into the atmosphere. The gases surround the Earth and keep heat in.

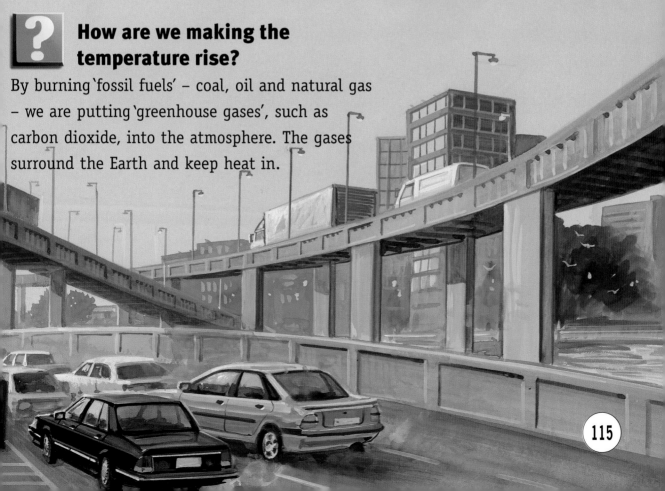

❓ What will happen as the temperature rises?

As the Earth's climate warms up, glaciers and the ice at the North and South Poles will melt, causing the sea level to rise. This will bring floods, and some islands will disappear. Deserts will spread, and droughts will occur.

Amazing! Cows are making the temperature rise. The smelly greenhouse gas methane comes from animals, such as cows, and from factories. Humans make it, too!

How can governments reduce carbon dioxide levels?

Burning petrol in cars puts carbon dioxide into the atmosphere. Governments can build transport systems that don't make carbon dioxide, and order more trees to be planted.

Electric railway

What can I do to help?

Use less electricity. This is because most electricity comes from burning fossil fuels which makes carbon dioxide. Switch off lights, TVs and computers when not in use.

Is it true?
If the Antarctic ice sheet melted, the sea level would rise.

YES. It holds two-thirds of the Earth's fresh water. If it melted, the sea would rise by up to 70 metres. Coastlines would change all over the world.

Antarctica

What other problems are caused by burning fossil fuels?

Sulphur dioxide is another harmful gas that comes from power stations and vehicles. It is very acidic, which means it eats things away. In the atmosphere, it mixes with droplets of moisture to make acid rain. Trees die when acid rain falls on them and on their soil.

Is it true?
Some polystyrene burger cartons are bad for the Earth's atmosphere.

YES. Some of them are because they're made using chemicals that damage the ozone layer. Many cartons are now made without these harmful chemicals.

Scandinavian forest damaged by acid rain

? Is Earth's atmosphere being harmed?

There is a layer of helpful gas around the Earth called ozone. It protects us from the Sun's dangerous ultraviolet rays. Unfortunately, the ozone layer is damaged because humans have put harmful chemicals into the atmosphere.

! Amazing!
When a nuclear power station at Chernobyl, Ukraine, exploded in 1986, radioactive material was sent into the atmosphere. Animals across Europe were contaminated by the radiation.

WARNING!
Always use a sunscreen in sunny weather to protect your skin from the Sun's rays.

? Is nuclear power dangerous?

Nuclear power stations do not burn fossil fuels. Therefore, they do not make harmful gases. But they do make radioactive waste material. It is dangerous and will have to be guarded for many years into the future.

Underground storage of nuclear waste

? Are there alternatives to fossil fuels?

There are other ways to make power. Solar panels collect energy from the Sun. The spinning propellers of wind turbines collect energy from the wind. Each of these energy-collectors makes electricity.

Wind turbines convert energy from the wind into electricity

Amazing! Cars can be powered by all sorts of things – solar power, gas, and even chicken droppings!

Are there any other types of natural fuel?

In many countries small amounts of energy come from rotting plants and animal dung. The methane they give off is burned to provide light and heat. This type of fuel is called bio-gas.

Bio-gas plant in India

Are these fuels better for the Earth?

Yes, they are. Solar power, wind power and bio-gas are cleaner, or 'green', forms of energy. They don't make harmful gases. They don't pollute the atmosphere. They don't make acid rain. They don't harm the ozone layer.

Is it true?
Electricity can be made from water.

YES. Running water is used to make electricity. This is hydroelectric power. The electricity is made by power stations built in or near dams.

Hoover Dam, USA

![?] Are animals in danger?

Thousands of different animals live on Earth. It is their planet, as well as ours. Sadly, because of what we do, many animals are in danger. An oil spill at sea harms seals, birds and fish. When forests are cut down, many animals lose their homes.

Oil spill

![?] How many kinds of animals are in danger?

There are many thousands of different kinds of animals in danger. Some are so rare they are endangered. This means they are almost extinct – they have almost died out. If that happens, they will have gone forever.

Endangered species

What is being done to save animals?

Many endangered animals are now protected by law. It is wrong for people to harm them, or the places where they live. Some endangered animals are bred in zoos. This helps to increase their numbers.

Golden lion tamarin

 Is it true?
Humans are causing animals to die out.

YES. It's said that one kind of animal dies out every 30 minutes because of what we're doing to the planet.

Cormorant covered in oil

 Amazing!
Passenger pigeons used to form flocks of millions of birds, but they were hunted to extinction in the wild. The very last one, named Martha, died in 1914.

123

Why do people kill certain animals?

Animals are killed for lots of reasons. Birds are killed for their colourful feathers. Elephants are hunted for their ivory. Tigers are killed for their skins. It's against the law, but it still goes on.

Stuffed animals

 ### Amazing!
Every year around 100 million animals and plants are taken without permission from the wild. It is because of this that they are endangered.

Collecting rainforest plants

❓ What about plants?

Like animals, plants can die out too. More than 30,000 different kinds of plants are in danger all over the world. Collectors take them from the wild, or pay local people to do it for them.

Is it true?

Sea turtles are hunted for their shells.

YES. Even though it's illegal, sea turtle shell, called tortoiseshell, is still used to make spectacle frames and souvenirs for tourists.

Illegal animal goods

❓ What can I do to help?

Don't buy goods made from ivory, fur, coral or tortoiseshell. Don't pick or dig up wild plants. If you eat tuna fish, make sure it's dolphin-friendly. Dolphins die in some fishing nets.

Rainforest

Why are forests good for the Earth?

Forests are the 'lungs' of the planet. Their trees make much of the oxygen we breathe. Forests provide us with food and timber. Some medicines are made from plants found only in forests.

? Are forests in danger?

Forests are in danger in many parts of the world. In some countries trees are killed by acid rain. Elsewhere, whole forests are cut down for their timber, or to make way for farm land.

Logger truck

What is being done to save forests?

Some governments have stopped cutting down the forests on their land. Many forests that are left are protected by law. Also, new forests are being planted, to grow timber like any other crop. It is grown to be cut down.

Amazing! Since 1980, an area of tropical forest six times the size of France has been turned into farm land, or plantations of oil palm, rubber and other crops.

Is it true?
Soil erosion can be seen from space.

YES. Trees keep soil in place. Where forests are cleared the soil wears away, or erodes, until only rock is left.

Soil erosion on Madagascar, seen from space

How much rubbish do people make?

Too much! People make rubbish and every household makes lots of it every day. In Britain, every family makes about 1.75 kilograms of rubbish each day. Over one year that adds up to more than half a tonne of rubbish!

Is it true?
Some rubbish is dumped at sea.

YES. Every day thousands of tonnes of rubbish are thrown into the sea. The seabed is littered with rubbish, such as bits of plastic, that never rot away.

Rubbish dump

Rubbish dumped at sea

❓ What happens to all this rubbish?

Because so much rubbish is made, it's a problem to deal with it all. Some is burned inside furnaces. A lot is buried on the land. Some rubbish is collected and sent for recycling.

Burning rubbish in a furnace

 Amazing!
The world's rubbish mountain grows by about 2 million tonnes every day.

❓ What can I do to make less rubbish?

Put the three Rs into practice: Reduce, Reuse, Recycle. Reduce means use less of something. Reuse means use something again. Recycle is to save something so it can be made into a new thing.

? What can I do with glass?

When glass bottles and jars are empty, wash them out and take them to a bottle bank. Most supermarkets have them. When they are full, the glass is taken to a factory where it is crushed, melted and made into new bottles and jars.

Amazing! Around 6 billion glass bottles and jars are used in Britain every year, but only three out of every ten are recycled.

Bottle bank

? What can I do with plastic?

Some kinds of plastic can be recycled. It can be turned into material to make plastic parts for cars. Plastic bottles for fizzy drinks are often made of recyclable plastic. These bottles can also be reused, by being made into useful items.

Reused
plastic bottles

Paper recycling

? What can I do with paper?

Most paper can be recycled, from newspapers and telephone directories to sweet wrappers and envelopes. It is made into new paper and cardboard.

Is it true?
Glass can be recycled over and over again.

YES. You just keep on crushing it, melting it and making it into new bottles and jars.

131

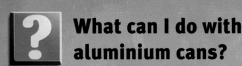

? What can I do with aluminium cans?

Cans and tins that hold fizzy drinks and even sardines are often made from a lightweight metal called aluminium. Look for the ALU symbol on them. They can be melted down and made into new cans.

Reusing clothes

Amazing! In Britain we throw away around 11 million aluminium cans every day. If you think that's a lot, the USA throws out 200 million!

132

Can recycling

Using magnets to test cans

What can I do with steel cans?

Most food cans are made from steel. A magnet will stick to a steel can. If it doesn't stick, the can is probably made from aluminium. Wash the cans out and take them to a can bank. Steel is the world's most recycled material.

Is it true?

Christmas trees can be recycled.

YES. Real Christmas trees (not plastic ones!) can be cut into tiny pieces, called chippings, which are used by gardeners.

What can I do with old clothes?

Give old clothes to charity shops. They are sorted out and many are sold as second-hand clothes. Some old clothes are sent abroad. Tatty clothes are sent to textile mills where they are ripped to pieces and used to make felt.

What can I do with kitchen and garden waste?

Vegetable peelings, tea leaves and grass cuttings are 'green' waste. If you pile them into a heap in the garden, they will rot down to make compost.

Even some kinds of paper can be turned into compost

Why is compost good for the environment?

Compost is food for the soil. It contains nutrients (foods) which keep soil healthy. Using home-made compost means less peat compost is dug up from natural places, and animals' homes are saved.

Gardening with compost

Are there other ways of recycling green waste?

You don't need a garden to recycle green waste! You can make small amounts of compost and plant food inside a wormery – a container where a colony of worms live. Worm bins can be kept inside or outside.

Is it true?
Leaves make good compost.

YES. Leaves rot down slowly to become leaf mould. Put them in a black bag or an open-topped wire cage. After two years you'll have compost.

Amazing! Green waste in a rubbish tip makes dangerous methane gas, and liquid that can pollute water and kill wildlife. It's safer to make it into compost.

Polluted river

Are there any dangers to our food?

Some people are worried about genetically modified (GM) foods, where the genes – instructions – have been changed by scientists. Because this has not happened in nature, no one knows how safe these foods are.

Spraying crops with chemicals can harm the delicate balance of nature

Amazing! Pollen from crops that have had their genes changed can mix with organically grown crops. When this happens, an organic crop is no longer organic.

What does 'organic farming' mean?

It's a natural way of farming where crops are grown and animals raised without using man-made chemicals. Also, the plants and animals have not been changed in any way.

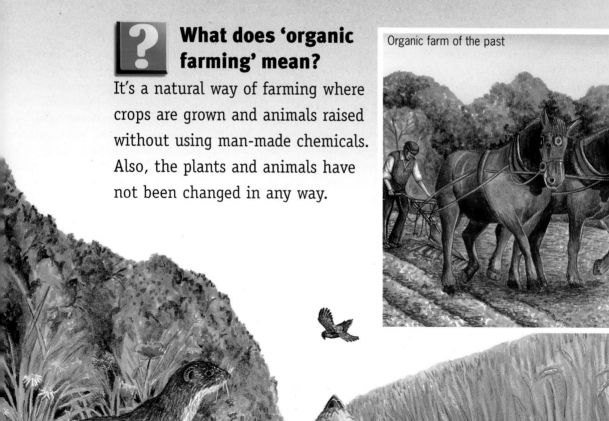

Organic farm of the past

GM crops need fewer pesticides.

YES. Scientists are changing the genes inside some crops so that they can resist diseases and pests on their own.

What can I do about it?

It's easy, and fun, to grow some foods at home, such as cress and tomatoes. Be organic, so don't put any chemicals on them. They'll taste good!

Tomato growing

137

What can I do at home?

Inside the house, start your own recycling centre, collecting materials that can be recycled. Reuse carrier bags, switch off electrical items when they're not in use, and don't leave taps dripping. Outside, get composting, and grow your own organic vegetables.

Energy-efficient house

Insulation to keep the heat in

Switch off electrical items after use

Don't leave taps dripping

Amazing!
Even an alien would think Earth needs caring for. That's because there are 100,000 pieces of space junk whizzing around the planet.

Cycling is energy- efficient and good exercise

Grow your own organic vegetables

Green Club

❓ What can I do at school?

If your school has a Green Club, join it. If it doesn't, ask if one can be started. As at home, switch off lights when they're not in use, and collect paper, cans and glass for recycling. Walk or cycle to school. Try to use cars less.

Sorting rubbish for recycling

❓ Is it true?
You can make a difference.

YES. Imagine if everyone in your class, your street, even your town recycled things. What a difference that would make!

❓ How can I find out more?

If you would like to help make the Earth a better, safer place to live, now and in the future, you might like to join groups such as Greenpeace, Friends of the Earth or World Wide Fund for Nature. Your library will have their addresses.

Sort your rubbish for recycling

(139)

Glossary

Acid rain Rain that contains chemicals which are harmful to nature.

Active volcano A volcano that is still erupting.

Algae Tiny plants that live in water.

Amber Once liquid tree resin (sap) which has been fossilised.

Amphibian An animal that lives on land and in water, such as a frog.

Atmosphere The gases or air surrounding a planet.

Bacteria Tiny, living things that live in soil, water and the air.

Bark The tough protective outer layer of a tree, which covers and protects the trunk and the roots.

Blizzard A winter storm with strong winds and heavy snow.

Butte A small, flat-topped hill in the desert.

Carnivore An animal that eats only meat.

Climate The weather conditions in a particular place on Earth.

Coniferous Trees which have needle-like leaves and cones, such as cedar, fir and spruce trees.

Crust The solid layer of rock on the surface of the Earth. It is about 8 km thick under the sea, and 40 km thick under the continents.

Cumulonimbus Another name for a tall, dark thundercloud.

Cynodont A type of reptile with fur, which evolved into mammals.

Dam A barrier built across a river to stop it flooding or to collect water in a reservoir.

Delta The end of a river where it flows into the sea.

Dinosaur A type of reptile that once lived on Earth, but which has died out.

Dormant volcano A sleeping volcano that could erupt at any time.

Drought A time of very dry weather when less rain than normal falls.

Equator The imaginary line which

runs around the middle of the Earth.

Extinct volcano A volcano that has stopped erupting.

Fault A crack in the Earth's crust.

Fold mountain A mountain made when one piece of the Earth's crust crashed into another and pushed up the land in between.

Fossil The remains of an ancient animal or plant preserved in rock.

Fossil fuels Fuels such as coal, oil and gas, made from fossilised remains.

Freshwater Water that does not taste salty. Rivers and many lakes are freshwater.

Genes The instructions that make living things what they are.

Greenhouse gas Gases, such as carbon dioxide or methane, which surround the Earth and keep heat in.

Habitat The surroundings in which an animal or plant lives.

Herbivore An animal that eats only plants.

Lava What magma is called when it erupts from a volcano.

Lightning conductor A rod on the roof of a tall building which is attached to a strip of metal. It carries electricity from the lightning safely down to the ground.

Magma Rock deep beneath the Earth. It is so hot that it has melted.

Mammal An animal with a backbone that feeds its young on mother's milk.

Mantle The part of the Earth between its crust and its central core.

Meander A large bend in a river. Sometimes a meander gets cut off and forms an oxbow lake.

Mesa A large, flat-topped hill in the desert.

Moon An object in space orbiting a planet.

Nuclear power Power made from radioactive material.

Nutrients Chemicals dissolved in water, used by plants in order to grow.

Omnivore An animal that eats both meat and plants.

Organic A living thing, or something made from a living thing.

Oxygen A gas that animals breathe in and which keeps them alive.

Peat A dark brown material made from rotten plants.

Poles The points at either end of a planet's axis, known as the north and south poles.

Prehistoric An ancient time before writing was invented.

Prey An animal which is killed by another animal for food.

Radioactive A substance that gives off harmful rays and particles.

Reservoirs Lakes used to store water.

Seasons Different times of the year, when Earth's weather and life change according to the position of the Sun in the sky.

Soil erosion Wearing away of the soil.

Solar panels Mirrors that capture energy from the Sun and turn it into electricity.

Solar power Power made from the Sun.

Solar System Our Sun and everything that travels around it.

Stalactite A spike made of stone which grows downwards from the ceiling of a cave.

Stalagmite A spike made of stone which grows upwards from the floor of a cave.

Submersible An underwater vehicle like a small submarine.

Tarn A small mountain lake carved out by ice millions of years ago.

Twister Another name for a tornado.

Ultraviolet rays Harmful rays from the Sun.

Index